FOCUS ON DISASTERS

Earthquake

Fred Martin

RIGBY
INTERACTIVE
LIBRARY

Designed by Raynor Design

Produced by Mandarin Offset Ltd.
Printed and bound in Hong Kong

99 98 97 96 95
10 9 8 7 6 5 4 3 2 1

ISBN 1-57572-021-3

Library of Congress Cataloguing in Publication Data

Martin, Fred. 1948–
    Earthquake/Fred Martin.
            p. cm.–(Focus on Disasters)
    Includes index.
    Summary: Examines how and why earthquakes
    happen, their effects upon people and the
    environment, and what is being done to
    prevent future devastation.
    ISBN 1-57572-021-3 (lib.bdg.)
    1 Earthquakes–Juvenile literature.
    [1. Earthquakes.] I. Title. II. Series.
    Martin. Fred. 1948– Focus on Disasters.
    QE521.3.M34 1996
    363.3'495–dc20   95-38386

Acknowledgments
The Publishers would like to thank the following for permission to reproduce photographs:
Martin Adnum: p. 40; Associated Press: p. 41; British Geological Survey: p. 42; Frank Lane Picture Agency: p. 26; Frank Spooner Pictures: pp. 16, 18, 22, 23, 32, 35, 45; GeoScience Features: p. 34; Hulton Deutsch Collection: p. 5; Illustrated London News Picture Library: p. 38; J. Allan Cash Photo Library: p. 12; Michael Jay: pp. 6, 7, 31; Magnum Photos/Raghu Rai: p. 43; Popperfoto: p. 4; Press Association: pp. 27, 33; Lara Regan/SABA/ Katz Pictures Ltd: p. 19; Rex Features: p. 25; Rex Features/Al Jawad Sipa: p. 15; Science Photo Library: pp. 9, 11; Science Photo Library/David Hardy: p. 29; Science Photo Library/David Leah: p. 24; Science Photo Library/David Parker: pp. 36, 37; Science Photo Library/Peter Menzel: pp. 30, 44; The Shropshire Star: p. 39; Topham Picturepoint: p. 28; Zefa UK Limited: p. 8.

Cover photograph © Rex Features

The Publishers and Author would like to thank the *Guardian* for the extract from the article "An awesome shudder like the end of the world" by Dennis Kessler, 01/18/1995 which appears on p. 4.

Contents

A Century of Disasters

EARTHQUAKES are to be feared. Every year, many people die as a result of the enormous damage they cause. At their worst, earthquakes can cause some of the greatest **natural disasters**. There are at least two large earthquakes every year as well as thousands of smaller **tremors** that shake the ground. Few earthquakes are predicted in a way that gives people any real warning.

There are records of earthquakes for as far back as people could write and draw. It seems likely that the ancient city of Troy was destroyed by an earthquake about 3,000 years ago. Earthquake disasters have continued through every century, sometimes with great loss of life. In 1755, about 30,000 people were killed when the city of Lisbon was badly shaken. In the 19th century, major earthquakes occurred in India, Japan, Italy, and in the countries of Central and South America. All of them struck without warning, but all occurred in areas that have a long history of earthquakes.

An awesome shudder like the end of the world

An eyewitness account by Dennis Kessler in Kobe, January 17, 1995

THE suddenness with which the earthquake struck was almost cruel. One moment we were fast asleep, an instant later the floor—the entire building—had turned to jelly. But this is no gently undulating, liquid motion. This is jarring, gut wrenching shuddering of awesome proportions. It is impossible to think straight.

You are in bed, the safest place in the world. Your bed is on the floor, what you used to think of as solid ground. And with no warning the world has turned into a sickening roller-coaster ride, and you want to get off.

Possibly the most frightening part is the sound. This is not the dull rumble of thunder. This is a deafening, roaring sound, coming from everywhere and nowhere, and it sounds like the end of the world. It is terrifying.

—The Guardian, January 18, 1995

Photo Notes

- Kobe, a port city in Japan, was struck on January 17, 1995, by an earthquake that measured 7.2 on the Richter scale.
- Over 5,000 people were killed, and billions of dollars of damage was done.
- Despite advanced earthquake-proofing, some buildings and roads, like this double-decker expressway, collapsed.

Photo Notes
- The remains of San Francisco after the earthquake in 1906.
- Buildings were wrecked by the earthquake, but much of the city was destroyed by fires that started as a result of the shaking.
- People in San Francisco are still waiting for the next earthquake on the same scale as the one in 1906.

The Last 100 Years

At the start of this century, the earth's population was about one billion. Now it is almost six billion and still rising. Cities have grown and more people live in country areas. Many of them live in areas with a history of earthquakes, so an even greater human disaster is likely.

Some big cities are at risk. In 1906, much of San Francisco was destroyed when an earthquake shook the city and fires broke out. Tokyo was badly shaken in 1923, and Mexico City has been rocked several times. Other smaller cities such as Skopje in Macedonia, Agadir in Morocco, and Managua in Nicaragua have been scenes of major disasters. One of the worst was in 1976 when about 650,000 people died in the industrial city of Tangshan in China.

The power of an earthquake can be seen by what it can do to the ground. In 1964, one of the most powerful earthquakes in this century hit the town of Anchorage, Alaska. Streets were split apart and part of the land was raised up by 36 feet. Land was shaken like jelly, causing landslides. Giant waves from the sea completed the damage. It is hard to build anything to survive an earth movement like this.

Whether in cities or in country areas, living in a known **earthquake zone** becomes part of people's way of life. Every time there is an earthquake, the damage is repaired and new lessons are learned about how to survive the next big one, but everyone hopes that it will strike somewhere else.

DID YOU KNOW?

One of the first pieces of equipment to record earthquakes was made in China in about A.D.130. When the equipment was shaken, a ball dropped from one of eight dragons' mouths on the rim of a round bowl into a toad-shaped cup below. This showed the direction of the earthquake.

Moving Rocks

IT is easy to find proof that the ground we walk on is not as steady as it seems. Look at any place where layers of rock are exposed. A cliff by the coast is a good place to start. Look for lines in the rock and check to see if they are straight. There is a good chance that they are not. If they are broken or bent at an angle, this is proof that in the past they were moved by some great force. That force may have caused earthquakes.

Layers of Rock

Most of the rocks we walk on are made of small pieces that have been compressed together. These pieces have come from other older rocks or from the remains of plants or animals. Rocks formed in this way are called **sedimentary rocks**. Plant and animal remains can sometimes be preserved as fossils in sedimentary rocks.

Some **sediments** are washed down rivers and dropped on the sea bed. Others are the remains of ancient sea life that died and fell to the sea bed. Sedimentary rocks can also be formed when the sea level rises and the land becomes submerged under many layers of mud.

Limestone is one type of sedimentary rock. The pieces that make up limestone were once the shells and other remains of sea creatures that died and fell to the bottom of the sea. These sediments were laid down in flat layers one on top of another. Layers of rock like this are called **strata**. One layer can take thousands of years to form, as sediments slowly pile up on top of each other.

Folded and Faulted

The layers of sediments do not usually stay in horizontal layers. They are squashed from above, pushed up from below, and squeezed from both sides. This happens over the many millions of years that make up **geological time**.

The forces that act on the rocks are able to bend them, like a finger pushing on paper. A bend in the rock is called a **fold**. The earth's highest mountain ranges were formed in this way, as layers of sedimentary rock were folded. This explains why fossil remains of sea creatures can often be found near the tops of mountain ranges such as the Alps and the Himalayan Mountains.

Photo Notes
- Layers of sedimentary rock on a cliff.
- The layers have been broken along a line called a fault line.
- Great forces in the earth have pushed the rocks and made them break.

Sometimes instead of being bent by folding, the layers of rock are broken. The effect is like breaking an arm. The two parts tear apart and move out of line.

When this happens to layers of rock, it is called a **fault line**. But unlike a broken arm, faulted rock does not mend. Instead, it remains as a line of weakness. If pressure continues to build up on the rocks, it will cause more movement. It is usually the rocks nearest to the fault line that are the first to move.

Folds and faults are simple evidence that great forces are pushing on the rocks. There are some parts of the world where these forces are more active than in others. These are the places where earthquakes can be expected. These movements are usually very slow and take place over a very long time. Most are so small that they cannot be felt. An earthquake only happens when the movement of the rocks is more sudden and much more violent.

Photo Notes
- Layers of limestone were bent into folds as the rock in this cliff was squeezed.
- Earth movements cause earthquakes when rock is moving to form folds and faults.

Some places stay active in this way for up to 100 million years. People have only been on the earth for about four million years, so these are lengths of time that are very hard for us to understand. Earthquakes have been happening since long before people existed and are sure to go on long after them.

DID YOU KNOW?

The Alps, Rockies, and Himalayan mountains have all been pushed up by folding. The folding started about 50 million years ago. The Himalayas are still rising slowly.

Moving Faults

Photo Notes
- The ground has split along a fault line.
- Rocks on one side of the fault have slid up to form a step in the ground.

THERE are fault lines in every part of the world. Some are in ancient rocks that were broken hundreds of millions of years ago. Others are more recent breaks, where forces in the earth are still making them move. There can be movement along fault lines of any age, but most are along those that are younger. A young fault line can be tens of millions of years old. Old fault lines may be hundreds of millions of years old.

Moves Along the Fault

Fault lines can be almost any size. Some are small breaks where the ground has shattered and moved by only a few inches. Larger fault lines go down several miles into the rocks and can stretch the length of a continent.

Layers of rock are faulted when they are pushed or pulled past their breaking point.

Strain builds up until the rock snaps to make a fault. After the first break, there is no more movement until enough strain builds up again. Forces act to move the rock, but friction and pressure act to stop it from moving. In the end, the strain becomes too great, and the rocks move again along the fault line.

In some places, forces act to pull the rock apart. This tension causes a break along a **normal fault line** where rock drops down on one side. The ground can drop as a step by a few inches or by several feet. If rocks keep moving along the fault line, a steep **escarpment** can form that is several hundred feet high.

Moves in All Directions

A second kind of movement happens when forces push on a rock from both sides. This makes the rocks on one side break and slide up over the other side. This is called a **reverse fault**. The effect on the landscape can be similar to what happens along a normal fault. A small step or a larger escarpment can show where the rocks have moved.

A third kind of fault is a **lateral fault**, when rock is moving sideways in two different directions. Evidence for this is seen when rivers suddenly change course at right angles. Their flow is continually disrupted as the rocks keep moving. Land on one side of the fault may spring up to form an escarpment, though most of the movement is sideways rather than up or down.

The rocks in some places are broken by very many fault lines. These can go in the same direction or cross over each other in all directions. Where tension is pulling the rocks apart, the ground can be broken by several parallel fault lines. The land between the faults can drop down to form a **rift valley**. Death Valley in California is one place where this has happened. Where there are even more faults, the land can drop along each fault line in a series of steps. This is **step faulting**. The southern part of the Rhine River flows through a valley formed in this way.

The largest of all fault lines are along the edge of large slabs of the earth's crust called **plates**. Whole continents and oceans sit on top of these plates. They move in all directions over the globe. They move toward each other, away from each other, and sometimes they slide past each other. The movement of these plates is what causes both the greatest number and the most violent of all earthquakes.

Photo Notes
- The San Andreas Fault in California.
- The escarpment shows the fault line.
- The ground is moving in opposite directions along the fault line.

Plates on the Crust

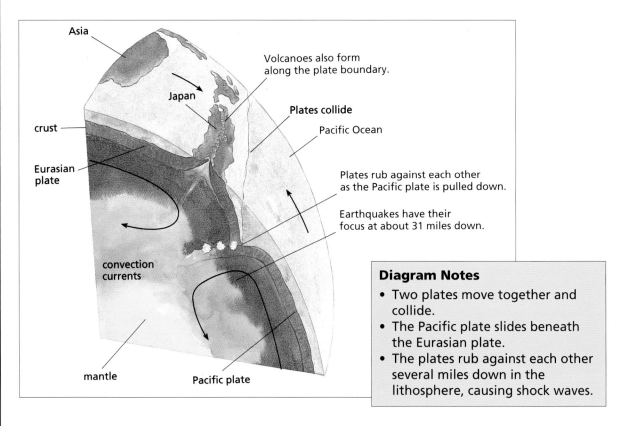

Asia

Volcanoes also form along the plate boundary.

Japan

Plates collide

crust

Pacific Ocean

Eurasian plate

Plates rub against each other as the Pacific plate is pulled down.

Earthquakes have their focus at about 31 miles down.

convection currents

mantle

Pacific plate

Diagram Notes
- Two plates move together and collide.
- The Pacific plate slides beneath the Eurasian plate.
- The plates rub against each other several miles down in the lithosphere, causing shock waves.

THE forces that move layers of rock cannot be found on or above the earth's surface. These layers are thousands of feet thick and have enormous weight. The wind, rain, ice, rivers, and oceans are able to shape the landscape, but they are not powerful enough to make the rocks in these layers bend and snap. The forces that do this are inside and beneath the rocks themselves.

The Earth's Layers

The earth's hard outer layer is called its **crust**. The crust is a thin layer—only between 3 and 30 miles deep. This is very thin compared to the 3,700 miles between the earth's surface and its center.

About 30 years ago, geologists discovered that the crust is not one solid piece. Instead, it is split into separate slabs that they call plates. These plates float like giant rafts on top of the layer beneath. The crust and upper part of the **mantle**, which is the layer below the crust, are the **lithosphere**.

About 300 million years ago, there was only one large continent that geologists have named Pangaea. Then the continent began to break up into separate plates. Since then, the plates have been moving about in all directions. Places that were once near the equator are now much further north. This helps to explain why there is limestone with fossils of coral in it in places where today it is far too cold for coral to grow.

There are now about 15 large plates and several smaller ones. They move very slowly at about 1 inch every year. This does not seem fast to us, but geological time is measured in millions of years.

This is fast enough to open up an ocean 1,250 miles wide in about 50 million years. The Atlantic Ocean has opened up in this kind of time. This explains why some of the older rocks, such as coal, are the same on both sides of the Atlantic Ocean.

Why the Plates Move

Something must be happening inside the earth to make the plates move. It is hard to find out exactly what this is because nobody can go there to study it. The **molten** rock from volcanoes gives some clues about what is under the crust. Shock waves from earthquakes give more information about what is there.

The inside of the earth is so hot that rock in it has melted. It is kept almost solid because the pressure is so great, but it is able to move very slowly. Currents of hot material move toward the crust from inside the mantle. When they reach the mantle, they separate under the crust and flow along in different directions. These are called **convection currents**.

The convection currents in the rocks are able to move the plates above them. As the plates move, they crash into each other, move away, or slide past each other. The pressures that cause these movements are enormous and cannot be stopped.

The plates do not move easily. The rocks send out **shock waves** when plates grind against each other. These vibrations are felt on the ground as earthquakes.

Sometimes, parts of the plates stop moving for a time. When this happens, they are said to be **locked**. When they are locked, the pressure to move builds up until at last the plates jolt forward again. All the energy is suddenly released, and there is a major earthquake.

There is a link between earthquakes and volcanoes. Both happen when the rocks are being torn apart or pushed together. Molten rock is able to come up through cracks and then flow as **lava**. The same forces that make the plates move also make volcanoes erupt.

Photo Notes
- Africa on the left is pulling apart from the Sinai Peninsula in the center of the photo.
- A major fault line between plates runs through the Red Sea and the Gulf of Aqaba to the right.
- A new ocean is slowly being opened up in this area.

Places at Great Risk

EARTHQUAKES have occurred in the same places throughout history as they do now. In the early 1990s, major earthquakes occurred in Turkey, Japan, India, and Iran. Nothing seems to have changed, though there is now more information about earthquakes in other places such as California and Indonesia.

The map below shows that there is a pattern to where earthquakes occur. This pattern helps to explain what causes earthquakes.

The Earthquake Belts

The first detailed map of where earthquakes strike was drawn by an Irish engineer named Robert Mallet. From 1830, he collected information about almost 7,000 earthquakes. Then he plotted their positions on a map. He knew that to understand why earthquakes happen, he had to know about the places where they happen. These places must have something in common.

There does not seem to be anyplace where the ground does not shake at some time. Small shakes are called tremors. These are very different from the more violent movements that are earthquakes.

Most major earthquakes are in lines that run around the earth. These lines are known as **earthquake belts**. Some of the earthquake belts run along the edges of continents. Earthquakes often shake the west coast areas of South America, Central America, and areas along North America's west coast. Another earthquake belt also runs through southern Europe and across into Asia. One of the most active earthquake belts runs through the mainland and islands along the western side of the Pacific Ocean.

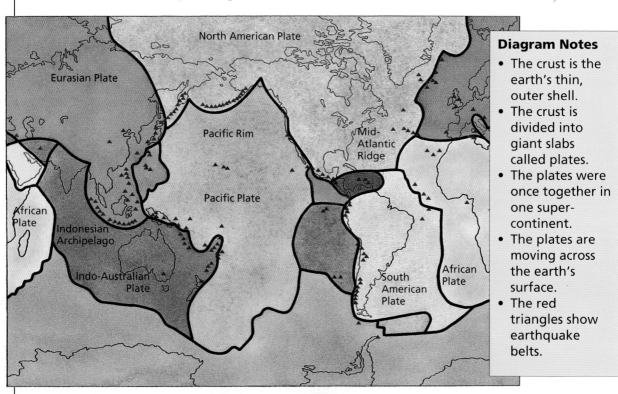

Diagram Notes
- The crust is the earth's thin, outer shell.
- The crust is divided into giant slabs called plates.
- The plates were once together in one super-continent.
- The plates are moving across the earth's surface.
- The red triangles show earthquake belts.

Photo Notes
- Tokyo is one of the world's largest cities with a population of 12 million.
- The city is in an earthquake belt where great damage has been done in the past.
- Imagine the damage that could be caused in this scene if another major earthquake struck without warning.

Plate Boundaries

Places where there are major earthquakes do have one thing in common. They are all near the edge of the plates that make up the earth's crust. Something is happening in these places that is causing the earthquakes.

Any movement of the plates shakes the ground in some way. Small tremors are usual where plates pull apart and lava oozes out onto the ocean floor. This happens down the middle of the Atlantic Ocean as the North American plate and the Eurasian plate continue to separate.

Along the west coast of North America, two plates are sliding past each other. The boundary line between them is called the **San Andreas Fault**. Tremors and earthquakes are also common in this area. One of the most recent was in 1994, when an earthquake in Los Angeles tore roads apart, damaged buildings, and caused broken gas pipes to catch fire.

The plates of the crust are colliding along the western side of the Pacific Ocean. Plates moving west are pushing into the large Eurasian plate. They keep moving by forcing their way under the Eurasian plate.

Volcanoes erupt along this line as molten rock forces its way up through the crust. In 1992, a severe earthquake struck Indonesia, killing almost 2,000 people. The plate movement and pressure caused by molten rock are more than enough to cause some very major earthquakes in this area.

In northern India, two plates are crashing into each other with neither one giving way. Rocks are being faulted and folded up into high mountains. All this movement also makes the area likely to suffer from earthquakes.

Some earthquakes do not follow the lines of plate boundaries. They happen where there are old fault lines that do not move very often. These can be very hard to predict because they are so unexpected. Some of the fault lines are not recognized until the earthquake happens.

DID YOU KNOW?

The number of people at risk from earthquakes increases every year as the world's population increases. People who live in cities are at the greatest risk because of falling buildings and fire.

Earthquakes Start Here

THROW a pebble into a pond and watch what happens. Ripples spread out from the center in waves. The pebble disturbs the water with the energy of its fall, and the ripples are caused by that energy. Earthquakes are caused by energy that is released when rocks suddenly move. The ground ripples, shakes, and can split apart as waves of energy spread out from where the ground has moved.

Deep Down

Some of the most violent earthquakes occur where one plate of the earth's crust is forced to slide under another plate. As this happens, a deep ocean **trench** is formed where the sea bed is broken and pulled down. The deepest ocean trenches occur where this happens along the coast of South America and in the western part of the Pacific Ocean.

As one plate moves down into the mantle, it grinds along the underside of the plate above. The place where this happens is called the **subduction zone**. The descending plate starts to break up and is melted by the heat in the mantle. Enormous amounts of energy are involved as the plate rock breaks up and melts. Rigid rock in the plate above can also be split by this movement.

The energy that is released is called **seismic energy**. The point where the energy is released is called the earthquake's **focus**. The focus for earthquakes can be as deep as 370 miles below the earth's surface. Most have a much more shallow focus, at about 30 miles down. A few are even closer to the surface.

Diagram Notes
- Earthquake shock waves start deep underground at the focus.
- Most earthquakes happen along the edges of plates.
- Seismic energy is released in ripples that spread up to the surface and also back into the earth.

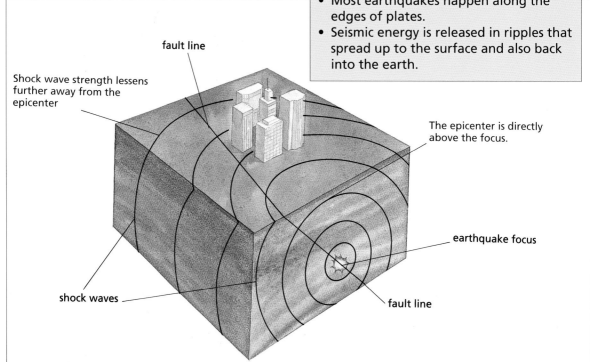

fault line

Shock wave strength lessens further away from the epicenter

The epicenter is directly above the focus.

earthquake focus

shock waves

fault line

Seismic Waves

Once the energy has been released, shock waves travel out from the focus. These are also called **seismic waves**. The waves travel in all directions, both toward the surface, and down into the earth. The point on the surface where seismic waves are strongest is directly above the focus. This point is called the earthquake's **epicenter**.

As more shock waves reach the epicenter, they spread out and ripple out over the surface. This is what cracks the ground and makes it heave. The strength of seismic waves fades away as they travel further from the epicenter.

The greatest amount of damage usually occurs nearest to the epicenter, although this is not always true. Shock waves have different effects on different types of ground. Rigid rocks are shaken less easily than rocks that are softer. Being on firm ground can be a greater advantage than being farther from the epicenter.

Before some earthquakes, small tremors are felt, leading up to the main shock waves. These tremors can happen for months, days, or only hours before the main wave. The main wave itself then arrives suddenly at a peak of strength. The ground can shake violently for only a few seconds as this peak passes. This is still usually long enough to reduce buildings to piles of rubble.

After the main wave, further smaller shaking can be expected. These are called **aftershocks**. People recovering from the main wave sometimes experience additional damage caused by aftershocks.

After the Alaskan earthquake in 1964, there were almost 300 aftershocks in the three days after the main shock. More smaller aftershocks were recorded for almost two years afterward.

Shock waves move in the same way when plates are pulling apart as when they are sliding past each other. The cause of the earthquakes is the same though the reasons for the movement are different.

DID YOU KNOW?

The deepest ocean trench is the Marianas Trench, which is 7 miles deep. The trench is where the western edge of the Pacific plate is sliding under the Indo-Australian plate.

Studying Shock Waves

PEOPLE have always been able to learn a little about earthquakes by looking at the damage they cause. Buildings that are knocked down or damaged show how strong the shock waves were. The direction from which the shock waves came can be determined by following the trail of damage and by looking at how the buildings were twisted. Until the shock waves could be measured, ideas about how they worked were vague.

Types of Waves

Seismic waves are measured on a **seismograph**. As the ground shakes, the movement is detected and recorded. This may be drawn by a needle on a revolving drum or may involve more modern electronic equipment. Some seismographs are small so that they can be carried to where earthquakes occur. Others are in permanent recording stations where they are able to pick up movements from all around the world.

Seismic waves move through the ground in different ways. The first type of waves to be felt are **P** (primary) **waves**. As P waves advance, the rock in front is pushed into the rock ahead. This is like a train colliding with a set of trucks.

Next come the **S** (secondary) **waves**. These roll the ground in a series of waves. They move up and down like waves in the sea, as the energy from the earthquake ripples out from its focus.

P and S waves behave differently in several ways. First, they travel at different speeds. The P waves travel through most rocks at about 3 miles per hour. S waves travel more slowly, at about 2 miles per hour.

A second difference is that P waves can pass through any kind of material, even through the hardest rocks. S waves can also travel through rocks, but they are unable to travel through liquids.

Some seismic waves on the surface, called **Love waves** and **Rayleigh waves**, roll the ground vertically and horizontally, as well as sideways.

Photo Notes
- A seismograph recording shock waves on a revolving drum.
- Information from shock waves helps find the earthquake's epicenter and measures the strength of the earthquake.
- Seismic waves also help scientists find out more about how to predict earthquakes.

Finding the Focus

The difference in speed between P and S waves can be used to determine where an earthquake has come from. Each type of wave is measured as it spreads out from the epicenter. The waves come quickly and close together at the epicenter.

As the waves travel further at different speeds, the time gaps between them become longer and longer. Think about two cars that start off together, then travel at different speeds in the same direction. They become farther apart the further they travel along.

When seismic waves are recorded at three places, circles can be drawn to show how far the waves have traveled. The earthquake's epicenter is where the circles meet at a single point.

Information from shock waves also helps scientists to determine what is under the earth's crust. Seismic waves travel back into the mantle as well as toward the surface. They are picked up by seismographs on the other side of the earth after traveling completely through it. The speed that seismic waves can travel through different types of rock is known. This makes it possible to figure out what kind of material the waves have passed through.

P waves are able to pass straight through the earth's core to places on the earth's surface directly opposite the earthquake. Some P waves are deflected off at an angle as they reach different layers inside the earth. This makes gaps called **shadow zones** where the waves cannot be measured.

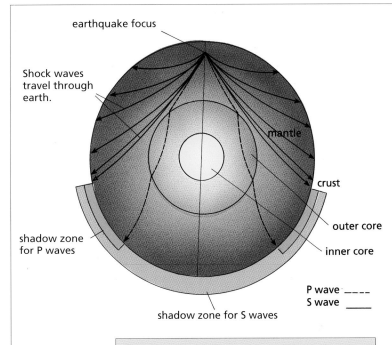

earthquake focus

Shock waves travel through earth.

mantle

crust

outer core

inner core

shadow zone for P waves

shadow zone for S waves

P wave ----
S wave ____

Diagram Notes
- Seismic waves ripple out from the focus toward the earth's surface and back through the interior.
- Shadow zones, where seismic waves are not felt, are caused as waves are deflected or when the waves cannot pass through a material.

S waves do not pass through the core. This must mean that the molten material acts like a liquid.

More information about shock waves is needed so that scientists will be able to make better predictions about when earthquakes are likely to happen. The information can also be used to design stronger buildings.

DID YOU KNOW?

Recording stations in countries all over the world measure seismic waves. These stations are linked so that they can share information. This is called the World Standardized Seismograph Network (WSSN).

Measuring Earthquakes

SCIENTISTS need to use mathematical figures to conduct their work. But how can the strength of an earthquake be measured? It is not like an experiment in a laboratory where everything can be carefully controlled. The amount of energy released during an earthquake is vast, and it goes in so many different directions.

Measure the Damage

One way to measure an earthquake is to study the amount and type of damage that it does. This was done by an Italian named Guiseppe Mercalli in 1902. He wrote a list of the kind of damage that could be expected after an earthquake. This was called the **Mercalli Intensity Scale**.

The Mercalli scale went from 1 to 12. In a gentle shake, only a few people would be able to feel anything. In a more violent shake, wood houses and even houses built of stone would be destroyed, roads and railroad lines would be broken, and rivers would burst their banks. A record of damage was made, then compared to what was written in the scale.

A problem with this scale is that the damage depends on how strong the buildings are. The type of rocks in an area and how accurately the damage is recorded also play a part. The Mercalli scale does not really measure the earthquake's energy. It only measures some of its effects.

To solve these problems, a new way of measuring earthquakes was invented by **Charles Richter** in 1935. His figures came from studying the height of seismic waves recorded on seismographs. He knew that the height of the waves decreased as they moved away from the source of an earthquake. This meant that the size of an earthquake could be measured from any recording station once the source of the earthquake was known.

Richter's Scale

Richter noticed that there was a great difference in the strength of earthquakes. Some were millions of times stronger than others. He wanted his scale to include all types of earthquakes, from the very smallest to the most powerful. To do this, he used a **logarithmic scale** instead of an arithmetic scale. An increase of 1 in the scale can show an earthquake that is 10 times stronger than the figure below it.

Photo Notes
- Damage to an Italian village after an earthquake measuring 6.8 on the Richter scale.
- The same earthquake gives a reading of about 10 on the Mercalli scale.
- The Mercalli scale has not taken into account how strong the buildings are.

So an earthquake measuring 6 on the scale is 10 times as strong as one measuring 5. Richter's scale measures the **magnitude** of an earthquake. This is a way of saying that measurements can be either small or vast.

News reports about earthquakes usually use Richter's scale to measure the earthquake's strength. A small tremor can measure 3 on the Richter scale. A violent earthquake can have a magnitude of 6 or 7. The 1964 earthquake that destroyed parts of Anchorage, Alaska, was measured at about 8.9. There is no limit to the scale. In 1992, one earthquake in the mountains of Kyrgyzstan near China was given a figure of 10. Figures of 5 and above are usually enough to cause widespread death and damage.

The Richter scale measures the amount of energy that is moved through the ground as seismic waves. But energy from earthquakes is used in other ways that are not so easy to measure.

A vast amount of energy is used when millions of tons of rock are heaved up along a fault line. More is used when rock is heated and broken by the movement. The total amount of energy from an earthquake is called its **seismic moment**. This is a figure that scientists now try to measure, as well as using the Richter scale.

DID YOU KNOW?

In an arithmetic scale, the numbers go up by the same amount being added on each time, for example, 2, 4, 6, 8. In a logarithmic scale, the figures go up by being multiplied by the same number each time, for example, 1, 10, 100, 1,000.

California's Earthquakes

Two of the world's plates meet in California, along a line called the San Andreas Fault that runs just inland from the Pacific Ocean. The Pacific plate is moving north while the American plate is moving past it to the south. This makes the conditions just right for earthquakes.

A Record of Quakes

The plates in California move very slowly. On average, they creep about 1.5 inches over a whole year. This is about the length of your thumb. **Seismometers**, which measure earthquakes, record about 10,000 tremors each year. Many are caused by small movements along smaller fault lines that also cross the area. Most are too small to be noticed by people. The ground only shakes when the movement is much larger.

California has a long history of earthquakes. In the last 200 years, there have been many major earthquakes. In 1857, the ground moved about 33 feet along the San Andreas Fault. In 1906, land along the San Andreas Fault line moved by up to 23 feet.

The 1906 earthquake destroyed most of the city of San Francisco. Wooden buildings collapsed and many of them caught fire. Since then, the city has been rebuilt and millions of people have come to live in California.

In some years, the plates hardly move at all. They become locked where the fault line changes direction and become wedged. Strain builds up in the rocks until all the energy is suddenly released. The plates suddenly jerk along the fault line.

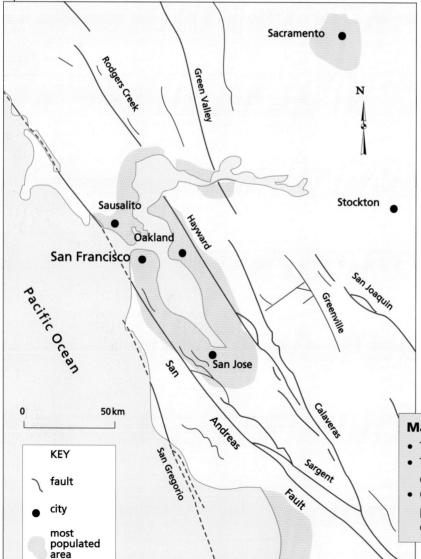

KEY

⌒ fault

● city

most populated area

Map Notes
- Two plates meet in California.
- The plates are moving past each other.
- Cities have been built near the plate boundaries and near the other fault lines.

They can move by several feet in a few seconds. These sudden movements can make living in California a risk.

A State at Risk

Since 1906, California has had many more earthquakes in different parts of the state. So far, none has matched the size of the 1906 earthquake. The largest earthquakes have cracked or destroyed buildings and broken up roads. Some damage is caused by **landslides** that were started by the earthquakes.

In 1989, another earthquake shook California. The epicenter of the earthquake was 60 miles south of San Francisco. It was a severe shake that measured 6.9 on the Richter scale. Buildings were shaken but few were seriously damaged. This is because they had been built to be stronger than those built in the past. However, some houses in the older districts were destroyed. Their wooden frames were simply not strong enough.

One stretch of road built on two levels suffered the most damage. In Oakland, the top deck collapsed and crushed people in cars on the lower deck. Rescue workers used dogs to find trapped people. In all, 67 people were killed and another 1,400 were injured. Others died as a result of heart attacks brought on by the shock of the quake.

California experienced another earthquake in 1994, this time in Los Angeles. Measuring 6.8 on the Richter scale, the earthquake caused 57 deaths and more than $15 billion in damage. In the weeks that followed, 5,000 aftershocks served as unsettling reminders of what had happened.

Geologists constantly measure land along the fault lines to check how it is changing. They are trying to predict when and where the next earthquake will occur. Some places are at greater risk than others, but accurate predictions still cannot be given.

DID YOU KNOW? [?]

Children in California practice earthquake drills in the same way that children in other states have fire drills. If the shaking starts when you are indoors, you must quickly get under a desk. Outdoors, get on the ground away from anything that might fall.

Photo Notes

- Damage during the 1989 earthquake in San Francisco.
- Steel and concrete supports have broken, and the top deck of the road has collapsed.
- Cars were crushed and people were killed.
- Supports will need to be made even stronger in the future.

Earthquakes in India

EARTHQUAKES have the greatest effects in countries where people are least able to protect themselves. Earthquake belts pass through some of the world's poorest countries, where they affect some of the world's poorest people. In these countries the death tolls are higher and problems for survivors are very severe.

Earthquake Disaster

Indians had no warning of the earthquake that struck in September 1993. Just the year before, India had suffered an earthquake that measured 4.5 on the Richter scale. People had been told not to worry—another one in the same area was not likely. The area near Bombay where the 1992 earthquake occurred is in the middle of the Indian plate. This is well away from places that are most at risk.

After the 1992 earthquake, the danger seemed to be over. People asked the government for help to build stronger houses, but they were ignored. A year later, an earthquake measuring 6.4 on the Richter scale shook the ground for 40 seconds. Two more large shakes followed but by then the damage was done. It was all over in a few minutes.

Houses Became Tombs

Between 10,000 and 20,000 people were killed in the earthquake. Some of the bodies will never be found.

Photo Notes
- Wrecked homes in the village of Khillari after the earthquake in October 1993.
- Roofs collapsed and trapped people who were in bed.
- Stronger houses would have helped reduce the number of deaths.

Nobody knows for certain how many people were living in the area. Most were crushed or suffocated when their mud and stone houses collapsed on them. In the village of Khillari, 6,000 out of 18,000 people died. It was the worst earthquake disaster in India in 100 years. One villager told a newspaper reporter, "The rising sun brought total darkness to our village, turning our houses into tombs." After the earthquake, heavy downpours of rain turned the ground to mud, making rescue work more difficult. The government sent the army to help, but India is a poor country. There are not enough hospitals, tents, helicopters, or bulldozers to cope with an emergency of this size. Poor roads made it hard to get to areas most affected.

When the army left, people were still homeless, and not all the bodies had been buried or cremated. Diseases such as cholera are a risk when this happens.

The cause of the earthquake may have been an old fault line that runs through the area. Full details of the rocks in India are not known, and there are not enough instruments to keep watch everywhere. People did not have enough money to make sure that their homes could survive an earthquake. It was also bad luck that the earthquake struck at night. During the day, nearly all the villagers would have been working in their fields. This earthquake struck people at most risk at a time when the most damage would be done.

Photo Notes
- Survivors hunt for trapped relatives in the rubble of their homes.
- Between 10,000 and 20,000 people died during the earthquake.
- Bodies had to be cremated quickly to avoid problems with disease.

DID YOU KNOW?

A traditional way to build houses in this part of India is to lay a thick layer of turf on the roof. This keeps out the cold, but it can collapse and suffocate people during an earthquake.

After the Earthquake

Some earthquakes cause damage on a scale that is hard to imagine. It is hard to think about numbers of deaths and injuries that run into thousands. The extent of earthquake damage is also hard to imagine when tens of thousands are made homeless and have their way of life destroyed. The scale of the damage is all too real for the survivors who have to pick up the pieces and start again.

Emergency Work

The immediate problems after an earthquake are easy to see. Rescue work has to take place in buildings that are likely to collapse on the rescuers. After the 1985 earthquake in Mexico City, some people who were trapped in collapsed blocks of apartments managed to stay alive for days before they were rescued. It is dangerous to use heavy machinery when there is still the chance of finding someone alive. Dogs and heat detectors are used to find anyone who is still alive.

Fires may have to be put out and rubble cleared so that the work of rebuilding can start. Emergency aid is needed to provide people with food, clothing, and somewhere to live. Cities of tents are erected for the homeless. Many different organizations join in to help.

Transporting supplies can be another problem. Bridges, roads, railroads, and airports can be destroyed.

There is a risk of disease from polluted water where pipes have broken and sewage mixes with drinking water. Water needs to be boiled, but people no longer have stoves. After a short time, another disaster might erupt somewhere else so help begins to dwindle. The work of rebuilding has to go on as best it can.

Into the Future

After the rescue work, it is a long-term job to rebuild what has been destroyed. About 200,000 new homes were needed after the 1993 Indian earthquake. Because people need jobs, farms, factories, and offices must be repaired. Some people want to stay and rebuild, but many others become **refugees**. They are too frightened to return or have no reason to go back.

Rebuilding costs money. The Indian government was given a loan of $450 million to help rebuild, but this money has to be repaid. Money spent on rebuilding cannot be used on other projects that might have improved people's standard of living.

A major earthquake that took place in Armenia in 1988 destroyed much of the town of Leninakan (now called Gumri).

DID YOU KNOW? ?

After the Indian earthquake in 1993, one problem facing rescuers was that thousands of people came to the site just to see the damage. They blocked the roads and got in the way. These people have been called "disaster tourists."

The death toll was 25,000, and tens of thousands were made homeless. Places of employment were also destroyed so people had to rely on aid and money from their government. After five years, many people were reported still to be living in boxes. Shops were still closed and there was a shortage of everything. Hospitals and schools were also closed.

Plans were made to rebuild the city, but little has been done. Political changes and war in the area have made it impossible to carry on the work.

Rebuilding after an earthquake is never easy. In countries such as India, Armenia, and others with a shortage of money, the problems are much greater. An earthquake can change people's lives forever.

Photo Notes
- The remains of Leninakan in Armenia.
- Most people in the town were left homeless and with few of their possessions.
- Years after the earthquake, houses still have not been rebuilt.

Unstable Ground

SOLID rock can split apart when an earthquake shakes the ground. Cracks open up, and land is thrown up and down in steps. Almost anything can happen when the ground starts to shake.

The chances of someone falling into a crack are very small. However, the chances of people being covered by a landslide are much greater.

Ground Like Jelly

Shock waves affect different types of rock in different ways. Hard rocks are jolted as the shock waves pass through them, but the shaking soon stops when the shock waves pass by. A special problem arises in places where the ground is less rigid. Layers of sand and other soft sediments often lie in the bed of lakes that may have dried up thousands of years ago. Mexico City is built on an ancient lake bed over soft layers of sediments. This is one reason why earthquakes have such a serious effect when they hit the city.

When these sediments are shaken by shock waves, they move more like a liquid than a solid. The loose materials are broken apart as the ground starts to shake. This is called **liquefaction**. Sand and water spurt into the air as they are squeezed out by pressure. Buildings sink down into the shaking sediments and are quickly destroyed. This is what happened to parts of Anchorage during the 1964 earthquake in Alaska. Houses sank into the ground where they crumpled like matchwood.

The Landslide Threat

Landslides are another risk in earthquake zones. The cause of these is seldom simple, although earthquakes frequently play a part. Rock is shattered from mountainsides by earthquakes, as well as by rain and frost. Some of the pieces lie where they have fallen. Other pieces fall down mountain slopes and come to rest as deep piles of loose rock.

Photo Notes
- Earthquake damage in Anchorage, Alaska, during the 1964 earthquake.
- The houses had been built on loose sediments.
- The earthquake shook the sediments and caused the house to collapse.

More problems can arise if this loose rock is made unstable by an aftershock or a second earthquake. Rainwater, too, can make the rocks unstable. Water lubricates dirt and mud and causes the material to slide. There is no way to judge when or where this is going to happen.

Landslides and mudslides bury anything that lie in their paths. They have caused many deaths in recent years in countries such as Colombia, Indonesia, and Nicaragua. Some landslides dump their rocks into rivers and cause flooding. This is what happened in Colombia in 1990, and again in Ecuador in 1993, when 30 people died and thousands were made homeless.

It is often hard to tell whether the earthquake itself or the rain is to blame for a landslide. However, it really makes little difference to the people whose lives have been affected. Some deaths, injuries, and damage from earthquakes could be avoided if homes and other buildings were put up only where it is safe to build, using information collected from past disasters.

People can add to the problem when trees and other vegetation are cut down from hillsides, exposing the soil to heavy rain. Without the soil to hold the rain, the threat of a landslide is even greater.

The dangers of liquefaction and of landslides are well known. Using this information could save many lives. People who ignore the danger take a risk.

DID YOU KNOW?

The Alaskan earthquake in 1964 was so strong that many recording instruments were unable to measure the size of the shock waves. The readings were too large for the paper on which they were to be recorded.

Tsunamis

DAMAGE from earthquakes does not come only as the shock waves rock the ground. People who live near the coast have another problem. This danger comes in from the sea, in the form of giant waves. They are sometimes called **tidal waves**, but they have nothing to do with the tide. They are caused by earthquakes that rock the ocean bed.

Killer Waves

In July 1993, news reports stated that 12 people had been killed and another 40 were missing after waves 16 feet high had swept onto the coastal area of Hokkaido. This is one of the group of islands that make up Japan.

As well as the deaths, about 40 houses were destroyed, and cars were swept away. Fishing boats were lost, and power cables were brought down. The waves had been expected, so the people were able to take sensible precautions to try to limit the deaths and damage.

The cause of the waves was a series of five earthquakes under the sea bed. The largest of these measured 7.9 on the Richter scale. Its epicenter was only 31 miles offshore. The sea had been rocked, and the waves had built up. Waves caused in this way are called **tsunamis**. An erupting volcano is also able to trigger a tsunami. The July 1993 tsunami was a small example of what one can do.

Tsunami Danger

Tsunamis are feared in all areas near the Pacific Ocean. There are thousands of islands in the Pacific Ocean, most of them low-lying coral islands where people depend on farming and fishing. In Japan, there is very little flat land except by the coast, so most of the population live there.

Photo Notes
- The effects of a tsunami on Japan's Hokkaido island.
- This tsunami followed an earthquake in July 1993.

The major cities of the west coast of the United States and Canada are all situated on the coast. The coast is also used for recreation, with summer homes built beside the beach. These places are all at risk from the threat of a tsunami.

An earthquake in any part of the Pacific Ocean can send tsunamis for thousands of miles. If the sea bed is faulted and heaved up, the water above it is also heaved up. This starts a tsunami.

At first, the waves are small, although they travel at around 500 miles per hour. As they reach the land, the water becomes more shallow. The waves slow down but grow in height. Just before the waves arrive, the tide seems to go out a little as it is sucked back. Then the biggest waves suddenly arrive. They can keep coming for several hours. At its worst, the tsunami can reach a height of more than 90 feet. Tsunami waves from the 1964 Alaskan earthquake reached Japan and California, causing more deaths.

A tsunami that struck Alaska during the 1964 earthquake was a very modest size at only 17 feet high. Boats were picked up and dropped in the middle of the town.

In the past, there has been no warning that a tsunami would strike. Now there are warning stations where earthquakes are recorded. One center in Hawaii sends information to other places around the Pacific coastline.

Although people now have better warning, tsunamis still cause deaths and destruction. Even with a warning, there is not much that anyone can do against a giant wall of water.

DID YOU KNOW?

In 1994, an earthquake started a tsunami that swept onto the coast of Hokkaido. Fortunately the people had been warned. There were about 140 injuries but only two deaths, both from heart attacks.

Building to Survive

THE amount of damage caused by an earthquake varies from place to place. The earthquake's magnitude affects the amount of damage, but this is not enough to explain why there are human disasters in some places and not in others. The greatest difference depends on the strength of people's homes and other buildings. People who live in countries that are rich are more likely to survive than people who have a much poorer standard of living.

The Right Foundations

One starting point is to know where to build. Most deaths and injuries during an earthquake are caused by buildings that collapse. Buildings need good foundations set into hard rocks. In hard rock areas, the ground shakes, but the shaking is soon over. The damage is worse where buildings are built on softer rocks or loose sand and clay. These areas shake for a longer period of time.

Mexico City is built on the site of an ancient lake. The buildings' foundations are on soft lake bed mud. People who live in tall blocks of apartments are especially at risk. In 1985, an earthquake shook Mexico City leaving 7,000 dead and about 30,000 homeless. Many apartments collapsed, killing those unlucky enough to be inside. It is too late now to build the city somewhere else. Better ways to build apartments will need to be found.

Another answer is not to build close to known fault lines. The land can be used in other ways such as for farming or outdoor recreation. However, this is not as easy as it sounds. Areas that can be affected cover many acres on either side of a fault line. Other fault lines may crisscross the area as well. Strict controls are needed on what is built where, but this is never easy. Controls such as these are especially difficult to enforce in countries where the people are poor and other problems seem greater.

Photo Notes
- Mexico City was hit by an 8.1 earthquake in 1985.
- Blocks of apartments collapsed when their foundations were shaken.
- The city is built on soft rocks that shake severely during an earthquake.

Building Design

A building's strength affects how much damage is done to it. In rich countries, only the strongest materials are used in areas where there are earthquakes. In poorer countries, homes may be built from cheaper materials such as wood and baked mud. People are likely to be buried as walls and roofs cave in.

A building's shape and how it is built can also help make it strong. A building that is too tall and rigid can snap when the ground shakes. If it can bend a little, it is able to absorb some of the earthquake's energy and survive.

One of San Francisco's tallest buildings has the shape of a slender pyramid. This makes it stronger. In some buildings, a type of rubber is used in the foundations. The shaking is absorbed before it moves up into the building. Buildings built on springs have the same effect.

In poorer countries, simple ideas can be used to make buildings stronger. A simple cube is the strongest shape. Corners need to be strong, so doors and windows need to be built away from them.

Photo Notes
- Tall buildings in San Francisco.
- The pyramid shaped-building is the Trans-American building.
- The pyramid design makes it strong enough to sway 40 feet so that it can survive a major earthquake.

Long stones should go through rubble walls to help tie them together. Roof supports should be firmly attached to the outside walls, with no weak points where part of the roof could collapse. Any new rooms that are added must be properly attached to the rest of the building. The earthquake is sure to pick out the weakest point first, so there must be no weak points.

It is also important to plan how a building is used inside. Loose furniture and objects on open shelves will be knocked down during an earthquake and cause injuries. Electricity and gas pipes must be made secure. If they break, fire can finish the job that an earthquake starts.

When all the precautions have been taken, there is nothing anyone can do except to wait. Ideally, nobody should be killed because they were not prepared and did not know what to do.

Planning for Disaster

Lives can be saved during and after an earthquake if people know what to expect and what to do. They must know where it is safest to be. Plans are needed so that emergency services can take over and keep the damage to a minimum. Above all, people must not panic.

Cairo's Lesson

An earthquake rocked the city of Cairo, Egypt, in 1992. Ancient buildings were cracked and new apartment houses collapsed. About 560 people were killed and 4,000 were injured. There was panic and confusion as people were trapped and others tried to get away. There was no warning of the earthquake, and people did not know what to do.

Cairo is a city of 15 million people. The number increases every day as more people arrive from the countryside.

Because Cairo has a shortage of houses, up to half a million people live on rooftops. Apartment houses have been built there, but these do not always meet building codes. Foundations are weak, and they are built too quickly and cheaply to survive an earthquake. People are not trained to cope with an earthquake emergency.

The situation in Cairo is typical of many other cities in countries where people have a low standard of living. Governments do not have enough money to provide basic homes, education, and other services. Little is left to plan and to educate people for an earthquake emergency.

Photo Notes
- Rescuers look for survivors trapped during the 1992 Cairo earthquake.
- People were not prepared for an earthquake and did not know what to do.

Japan Plans

Japan is one of the world's wealthiest countries. It is also a country where earthquakes and volcanoes are a constant threat. Most people live and work in cities on narrow strips of lowland along the coasts. They are at risk from earthquakes. This is why earthquake drills take place every year.

In Japan, September 1 is **Disaster Prevention Day**. This is the anniversary of the day in 1923 when a terrible earthquake struck the capital city of Tokyo. After the quake, tidal waves and fires swept the city, killing a total of 143,000 people.

At a designated time, everyone moves to the nearest piece of open land. Signs show them where to go. Volunteers get out emergency equipment to practice putting out fires and rescuing people. People are advised to keep their own emergency supplies at home. The police, hospitals, and fire departments all know what they have to do.

When a major earthquake does strike, the plans might not work as they do during a practice, which is expected. Planning and practicing what to do will help reduce the numbers of deaths and injuries.

A problem is that the plans depend on how much warning people can be given. If there is no warning, then many more people will be killed, and there could be another major disaster.

DID YOU KNOW?

In October 1994, a massive earthquake of 8.2 on the Richter scale shook Japan's Hokkaido Island. Fortunately the epicenter was 165 miles to the east in the Pacific Ocean. A 6-foot tidal wave crashed onto the shore, but damage was light. A similar-sized earthquake a few miles further west and south could have caused much more widespread damage.

Studying Earthquakes

PART of the job of a scientist is to be able to predict when, how, and why something will happen. Some scientists work in a laboratory, experimenting with small amounts of chemicals and other materials. They can carefully measure what they are doing and use accurate figures to explain what has happened.

Scientists who study earthquakes are no different. They try to predict when, what, and why earthquakes happen. But it is hard to measure earthquakes, and just as hard to make accurate predictions.

Studying the Past

The focus of an earthquakes lies deep inside the earth's crust. To understand earthquakes, geologists need more information about the area around a focus. But these areas cannot be visited—they are too deep, and it is too hot. Even if a hole could be drilled that deep, the measuring instruments would melt. Scientists must rely on shock waves for information about where and why earthquakes start.

Another problem is that scientists cannot make an earthquake in a laboratory so that they can study it. They have to wait until one happens.

Information about past earthquakes gives some clues to how often earthquakes may happen in the future. Rock movement along fault lines is studied to see how often layers have been disturbed. This provides an average figure for the time between earthquakes. An average, however, is not much use if each figure differs too much from the average.

There has not been a major earthquake in Lisbon since 1755. Scientists think there may be a gap of 200 years between earthquakes in Lisbon, but there were no signs of another one in 1955. This could mean that a major earthquake is now overdue and will happen soon, or it could mean that there will never be another one of the same size. There is no way to be sure.

Photo Notes
- Geologists study a fault line in Iran.
- There have been several major earthquakes in Iran in recent years.
- Information about past movements along fault lines helps geologists predict future earthquakes.

Earthquake Theories

Over the years, geologists have improved their understanding of how some earthquakes behave. The places at greatest risk are those where not much movement has been detected for a long time. Small earthquakes will occur as long as the plates keep moving. But when the ground does not move for several years, strain in the rocks builds up. Places where there has been little recent movement are called **seismic gaps**. These are places where geologists predict the next major earthquakes will happen. Still, they cannot predict exactly when.

Some scientists believe they can detect a quake before it strikes. They theorize that small shock waves are the first signs that something is about to happen. These **foreshocks** show that rocks are starting to crack under increasing strain. This can go on for a few weeks with times between when nothing seems to happen. Suddenly, the fault line jolts, and the energy from the strain is released.

Even if this is correct, the right kind of measurements must be made in the right places and at the right times. This is not always possible. Some places are hard to get to, both on land and beneath the sea. Scientific instruments are expensive and people are needed to read them. Only the richest countries can afford them, but every country needs to take measurements if more earthquake disasters are to be avoided.

DID YOU KNOW?

In 1976, Chinese geologists correctly predicted an earthquake that shook Liaoning Province. People were evacuated and there were few problems. Five months later, the city of Tangshan was shaken apart by an earthquake that was not predicted. This time, about 650,000 people were killed.

Measuring the Moves

SOME earthquakes seem to give no warning signs. The signs may be there, but it has not been possible to measure them. Possibly, scientists do not know what to measure. They do know that they have to find out as much as they can about how the ground behaves. They need to measure every movement and change they can detect. This is the only way to learn to make useful predictions about earthquakes.

Measuring Instruments

Earthquakes happen when the rocks are under so much strain to move that they suddenly jolt to relieve the strain. Strain in rocks is measured by a **strainmeter**. The problem is to know the point when the strain is too much to take.

Pressure on rocks to move sometimes makes them lift up or swell. This can be seen when slopes on the ground begin to change. The changes are very small, but sensitive instruments are able to measure them long before they are noticed by people. A **tiltmeter** is used to show how the ground's slope has changed. A tiltmeter 33 feet long is able to measure a change in angle that is one ten-millionth of a degree. A small change may be the start of something larger.

A **magnetometer** is used to measure how far the ground moves, by taking regular measurements of the earth's **magnetic field**. Readings from instruments on different sides of a fault line are compared to readings away from the movements. Any differences between them could show that the ground is moving. It may be just as important to know when it is not moving, as it is when the greatest strain builds up.

Photo Notes
- Measuring ground movement near the San Andreas fault line.
- The amount of ground creep is being measured to see if small movements give any clues about when a major earthquake will happen.
- A **creepmeter** can measure a movement of 0.001 inch.

Gravity, Lasers, and Animals

Everything on the surface is pulled down by the earth's gravity. This force can be measured on a **gravimeter**. If the land rises or falls, the force of gravity changes.

There is also a change if the density of rocks changes. This can happen if **magma** from the mantle starts to rise, or if the rock is changed in some other way. These changes may show that movements in the earth's crust are starting, and that an earthquake may be due.

Very accurate measurements about ground movements are found by using **lasers**. These are thin light beams that travel at 142,700 miles per second. This is the **speed of light**. A laser beam can be aimed at a target on the other side of a fault line, then reflected back again. The time taken for the beam to travel this distance can be measured because its speed is already known. If the ground has moved, the time taken for the beam to be reflected will change, and the amount of movement can be determined. Laser beams have been set up along the fault lines in California to make sure that any moves are recorded.

In China and Japan, animals are studied to see if they can sense earthquakes.

Small animals such as ants live in the ground, so they should be able to feel any slight tremors. They may also be able to smell changes to gases that come up through cracks in the rocks. Larger animals such as chickens, pigs, or pandas may also feel or smell these changes. If they are disturbed by the changes, they may change the way they normally behave. However, not all scientists think that studying animal behavior is helpful.

All these instruments help scientists to find out about how the ground is moving and changing. They hope that this information can be used to make better predictions about earthquakes. Better prediction is one of the most important ways in which disasters can be avoided.

DID YOU KNOW?

There is more earthquake-measuring equipment near Parkfield on the San Andreas Fault than anywhere else in the world. The plates are locked at Parkfield, but scientists think that this is where the next major earthquake will happen. They want to know exactly what happens before an earthquake so that they can predict the next one.

Earthquakes Everywhere

EARTHQUAKES happen everywhere and can occur at any time. On average, a powerful earthquake shakes the ground less than once every two years. About 40 moderate earthquakes cause damage somewhere in the world each year. And scientists say that about 40,000 to 50,000 small earthquakes—large enough to be felt, but not large enough to cause damage—also occur each year.

Most earthquakes occur near or along the boundaries of the rocky plates that cover the earth's surface. But on occasion, an earthquake can strike in an unlikely place, surprising many people. Even when people know they live in an earthquake zone, they usually are not prepared for the disaster that can be caused by a powerful quake.

Great Britain's Earthquakes

In 1884, nobody could have expected an earthquake in Colchester, a small market town near London. Residents were taken by surprise when the ground suddenly began to shake. The shaking lasted for about 20 seconds. The shock waves rippled out through nearby villages until they reached London. Several people were killed by falling bricks and masonry. In some places the ground cracked open.

Geologists have estimated that the Colchester earthquake was 7.0 on the Richter scale. This is the biggest known earthquake in Great Britain. Others have occurred in recent years, but none nearly the size of the 1884 earthquake.

Scientists are not surprised that there are occasional earthquakes in Great Britain. In Scotland and Wales there are ancient fault lines through some of the oldest rocks. There are also fault lines in ancient rocks that lie under the more recent rocks in the south and east of Great Britain.

The Kobe Disaster

In January 1995, an earthquake that lasted barely 20 seconds struck Kobe, Japan. Measuring 7.2 on the Richter scale, the earthquake left 5,090 dead and 300,000 homeless. In addition, it

Photo Notes
- Damage to cottages during the 1885 Colchester earthquake.
- Chimneys collapsed and caused injuries to people inside and outside the houses.

destroyed more than 70,000 buildings and caused serious damage to roads, water service, power lines, and other vital utilities. Even some buildings that were supposed to be "earthquake proof" did not withstand the intense shaking.

Japan lies on a very unstable part of the earth's crust. The land in the area is constantly shifting. As a result, the Japanese islands have about 1,500 earthquakes a year. Most of them are minor tremors that cause little damage, but severe earthqukes occur every few years. The Kobe earthquke was the worst to shake Japan in more than 50 years.

Estimates to rebuild the city of Kobe were as high as $4 billion. And it will not be easy. One official said, "This city is going to take 10 years to rebuild."

Earthquake Flattens a Russian Town

May 1995 brought the largest ever recorded earthquake to Russia. Measuring 7.5 on the Richter scale, the earthquake flattened the town of Sakhalin, just north of Japan. Most of the approximately 3,000 residents lived in poorly built apartment buildings. These buildings should have

been built better, because the area is a known earthquake zone. Barely a third of the town's people, about 1,000, survived the earthquake.

Geologists believe that drilling in the Neftegorsk region may have helped cause the earthquake to occur. In addition, they believe that some warning may have been possible if five of the six seismography stations of Sakhalin had not been closed in 1994 due to lack of government money.

Russian officials announced soon after the disaster that the town would not be rebuilt.

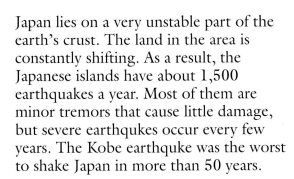

DID YOU KNOW? ❓

There were many earthquakes before the 16th century, but the records going back that far are not very good. It is difficult to be sure exactly what happened.

Low-Risk Areas

EARTHQUAKE belts run around the earth in great circles. Places away from these belts do not usually have earthquakes. They may have very minor tremors that cause little or no damage. When a rare, more violent earthquake happens, people are not prepared for it, and their buildings may not be strong enough to survive.

The First Death

The first recorded deaths from an earthquake in Australia were in December 1989. Newcastle is an industrial and mining town on the east coast of Australia about 95 miles north of Sydney. The town had no record of earthquakes. Most of Australia is made from old, stable rocks that rarely move at all.

The first shock waves came at 10:28 A.M. This was recorded at 5.5 on the Richter scale. The earthquake's epicenter was only a few miles to the west of the town. The shaking lasted for about 30 seconds. Some buildings in the town center were destroyed and others were damaged.

Photo Notes

- Rescue workers search for victims of the 1989 Newcastle earthquake in Australia.
- Buildings collapsed during a 5.5 earthquake that nobody had expected.
- Movement along old fault lines may have been caused by coal mining.

Eleven people were killed when buildings collapsed on them. Houses and shops in Newcastle's suburbs were also damaged. Shock waves were felt by people in Sydney.

Rescue work was made more difficult by the loss of power supplies and telephone cables. The ambulance and fire service buildings were also damaged.

The exact cause of the earthquake may never be known. Old fault lines run through the area, and rocks along these lines may have moved. A theory is that old coal mines may have weakened the rocks.

Rhineland Faults

The Rhine Valley is known to geologists as an area that has been shaped by faulting. Large blocks of land have been thrown up to form uplands. An upland block formed in this way is called a **horst**. The Eifel Uplands to the west of the city of Bonn is a horst block. Blocks of land have also slid down to form rift valleys called **graben**. This happened in Germany about 30 million years ago at the same time as the Alps were folded up. Rocks can move along any of these ancient fault lines, although none of them are very active.

In 1992, an earthquake measuring 6.3 on the Richter scale shook towns and villages on both sides of the Rhine Valley in northern Germany, the Netherlands, and Belgium. The epicenter was at Roermund, just north of the Eifel Uplands near Maastricht. About 200 houses were damaged during the 15-second shake. Some people thought that a bomb had exploded in Cologne, about 50 miles away. Injuries were caused in one town when people rushed outside to see what was happening. They were hit by falling bricks and glass. One person died of a heart attack caused by the sudden shock.

There is a history of earthquakes in the area but they are usually small and do not happen very often. They occur often

STOP PRESS Monday April 13, 1992, Herkenbosch, Netherlands. Report of earthquake at 5.5 on Richter scale. Large area of northern Germany and the Netherlands affected. Buildings shaken but little major damage or serious injury.

Photo Notes
- Shop workers clean up the damage after the April 1992 earthquake in northern Europe.
- Earthquakes are rare in this area, so no precautions are taken against them.

enough for people to remember that there is some risk, but not enough for them to ensure that houses are built more strongly and to have special plans in case one happens again. This is one reason why a small, unexpected earthquake can cause as much damage as a slightly larger one in an area where they are more common.

DID YOU KNOW?

After the Newcastle earthquake, an emergency services official said, "We never thought of ourselves as living in an earthquake area."

Starting Earthquakes

It is hard to know the exact amount of force needed to trigger an earthquake. In the past, it was thought that the force of the moon's gravity could pull on the rocks. Another idea was that earthquakes could be started by the extra weight of water when the tide came in. Now there are questions about whether people can play a part in starting earthquakes.

Mining and Blasting

People change the ground in many different ways. Minerals are quarried and mined, taking vast amounts of rock out of the ground. This is enough to cause land **subsidence**, but it is hard to prove that it can cause an earthquake. The 1989 Newcastle earthquake in Australia may have been affected by mining, but this cannot be proved.

Nuclear explosions shake the ground violently, but testing nuclear bombs is now a very rare event. Most countries have agreed not to carry out any more tests.

Large amounts of water, oil, and gas are taken out of rocks. The ground might move if the rocks become lighter, but there is no evidence that this really does cause earthquakes.

There is some evidence that putting water into the ground can cause a problem. This was discovered in Colorado in an area where polluted water was being pumped deep underground. Earthquakes increased as more water was pumped in. They stopped when the pumping stopped. There was a clear link between the two.

Building Dams

People put extra weight on rocks when dams and reservoirs are built. As a reservoir fills with water behind a dam, the weight of millions of gallons of water starts to press down on the rocks. The extra weight of water may be enough to make the ground more active and cause earthquakes. This is what seems to have happened after the Hoover Dam was completed across the Colorado River in 1936. The dam itself is a solid concrete wall 725 feet high. Lake Mead behind it stretches back for 115 miles and reaches 10 miles wide in places.

Photo Notes
- A hole in the ground caused by an earthquake in Scottish coalfield in 1986.
- Mining has disturbed the ground and may have caused the earthquake.
- There have been earthquakes in this area up to a magnitude of 2.8 on the Richter scale.

This is a vast and heavy amount of water.

The weight of the water may be only one of the problems. Some water seeps into the rocks below. This happens when rock is cracked, which it often is in earthquake belts. Water lubricates the layers of rock so it can move more easily. Without the water, the rocks may remain still for longer, or they may not move at all.

Some people are worried about a new dam to be built at Tehri, India, in the Bhagriathi Valley. This dam is planned to hold back about 1 cubic mile of water in a reservoir. In 1991, a severe earthquake struck the area near the dam site. Many people fear that the dam and reservoir will increase the risk of earthquakes in the area, and that the dam itself might not be able to survive a major tremor.

Geologists have thought of one way that water could help in areas where there are major earthquakes. Earthquakes are caused when the plates move, but there is no point in trying to stop them from moving. The worst earthquakes come after a time when they have not been moving. So it might be better if the plates could be helped to move, especially in places where they become locked. Water could be pumped into wells along the fault line to lubricate the rocks and help them move. People can cope with a small movement each year. It is the sudden, massive movements that cause most problems.

DID YOU KNOW? ?

One idea to keep plates moving along fault lines is to set off underground nuclear explosions. The dangers from doing this do not make this a popular idea, although it might work.

Earthquakes in the Future

EARTHQUAKES reflect the immense natural forces that shape the earth and affect the people who live on it. We must understand how to live with these forces if we don't want to be destroyed by them—they are far too great to control.

Science Fact and Fiction

The earth's plates have been moving around the globe for the last 300 million years. The force that pulls them along is inside the earth where it will remain until it cools down and becomes a dead planet. The plates on the map today will be much the same as the plates 10 million years from now. Some will be a little smaller at one edge where they are sliding under another plate into the subduction zone. There will also be some new areas of plate where lava has come up and cooled to form rock.

The places where earthquakes now occur will continue to have earthquakes. People who live in these areas have no choice but to learn how to survive their worst effects.

Scientists may be able to do something to keep plates moving in places where they become locked.

At the moment, ideas such as these are science fiction. The costs of doing them would be enormous. There would also be the risk of doing more harm than good.

Some progress will be made in understanding more about earthquakes. There will be better ways to measure and record how the rocks are behaving. Instruments may be put into the rocks in places where measurements cannot presently be taken.

Satellites are already taking measurements that show changes in the ground. These will be used to get information from places that are hard to reach, such as mountain areas. Deep-sea vessels will be able to take instruments to the ocean bed to find out what is happening there.

There are already instruments on the sea bed near Japan that give information about earthquakes.

Photo Notes
- There will be more earthquakes and more scenes like this when people lose their homes and have to start their lives again.

Living with Earthquakes

The danger of more human disasters from earthquakes increases every year as the world's population increases. The number of people could double in the next 50 years. More people will be crowded into larger cities. The population of Mexico City may increase to about 25 million by the year 2000. Mexico City has already been hit many times by major earthquakes, and more can be expected. There will be similar population increases in Cairo and other cities in known earthquake belts.

More people will live in country areas, in houses that have not been designed to survive an earthquake. Worst of all, the greatest increases will be in the world's poorest countries, where it is hardest to protect people from natural disasters.

New designs and materials are being tested all the time to find ways to build stronger buildings. These need to be suitable for people in both rich and poor countries. Better education will help more people to understand the dangers of living in earthquake areas and what to do when one strikes. Above all, accurate predictions need to be given so that people can take precautions. Scientists will need to find out far more about earthquakes before this can be done.

DID YOU KNOW?

The earth's population in 1960 was 2.5 billion. By 1990, it had risen to 5.3 billion. By the year 2000, the population is expected to rise to about 6.2 billion. Some countries such as Mexico will double their present population in about 30 years.

Glossary

aftershocks seismic movements that take place after the main earthquake

convection currents movement caused by heating, such as when magma is heated inside the earth and rises from the core toward the crust

creepmeter an instrument used to measure very small ground movements

crust the hard outer layer of the earth

Disaster Prevention Day September 1, a day in Japan when people practice how to survive an earthquake

earthquake a major shaking of rocks in the earth's crust

earthquake belt a broad band of land where earthquakes are common

earthquake zone an area where earthquakes are common

epicenter the point on the earth's surface immediately above the earthquake's focus

escarpment a steep slope along an area of upland

fault line a break in the rocks

focus the point in rocks where an earthquake originates

fold a bend in layers of rock

foreshocks small earth movements that are sometimes detected before a major earthquake

geological time very long periods of time during which rocks are formed

graben a depression caused when land drops down between fault lines

gravimeter an instrument to measure the pull of gravity

horst a plateau block formed when land is pushed up between fault lines

landslide a sudden and rapid movement of soil and rock down a slope

laser a type of light (Light Amplification by Stimulated Emission of Radiation)

lateral fault a sideways break in rocks

lava molten rock that comes to the surface from under the earth's surface

liquefaction a process during which soil that is shaken during an earthquake begins to move more like a liquid than a solid

lithosphere layers of the earth made from the crust and upper mantle

locked fixed in one place, such as when there is no movement along a fault line

logarithmic scale a way of arranging figures in a scale so that each increase is 10 times greater than the previous figure

Love wave a type of seismic wave that travels over the earth's surface

magma molten material beneath the earth's surface

magnetic field the area around a magnet in which it can attract other things

magnetometer an instrument used to measure magnetic fields in rocks

magnitude an index of measurement used to describe the size of an earthquake

mantle the layer between the earth's crust and the core

Mercalli Intensity Scale a way of measuring the size of an earthquake based on the damage it caused

molten heated until melted

natural disaster a great loss of life and injuries caused by forces in nature

normal fault line a break in rocks caused when the ground pulls apart

plates large slabs of the earth's crust

P waves primary waves; the first shock waves that come from an earthquake's focus

Rayleigh wave a type of seismic wave that travels over the earth's surface

refugee someone made homeless by a disaster

reverse fault a break in rocks caused by compression

Richter, Charles a scientist who invented a scale to measure the size of earthquakes

rift valley a valley caused when land slipped down between fault lines

San Andreas Fault a major fault line between two plates, mainly in California

sediment material that has been eroded then dropped

sedimentary rock a type of rock made from bits of other rocks or from the remains of ancient plant and animal life

seismic energy the energy released during an earthquake

seismic gaps places along earthquake belts where there has not been a major earthquake for a long time

seismic moment a measurement of the total amount of energy released during an earthquake

seismic waves waves of energy that spread out during an earthquake

seismograph an instrument used to measure and record earth movements

seismometer an instrument used to measure earth movements

shadow zone parts of the earth's surface where seismic waves cannot be recorded

shock waves (*see* seismic waves)

speed of light the speed at which light travels

step faulting a series of fault lines close together that move rocks by different amounts

strain the build up of energy in a rock

strainmeter an instrument used to measure the amount of strain in a rock

strata layers of rock

subduction zone the area where one plate has moved beneath another plate

subsidence ground that has collapsed

S waves secondary waves; the shock waves from an earthquake that come after P waves

tidal waves (*see* tsunami)

tiltmeter an instrument used to measure the angle of a slope

tremor a minor shake of the ground

trench a very deep part of the ocean bed, usually where one plate is sliding beneath another plate

tsunami exceptionally high sea waves caused by the movement of the sea bed during an earthquake or volcanic eruption

Index

Earthquakes mentioned in this book are printed in bold.